I0786460
Happy Birthday
Sister!

DEAREST SISTER,
YOU ARE THE BIRTHDAY GIRL!

PARTY TIME!

SISTER,
LET'S CELEBRATE!

TODAY IS THE DAY TO BE HAPPY!

SISTER,
YOU ARE AMAZING!

CHEERS!

FABULOUS SISTER, IT'S YOUR SPECIAL DAY!

HIP! HIP! HOORAY!

SISTER,
IT'S YOUR BIRTHDAY!
MAKE A WISH!

BELIEVE IN MAGIC!

SWEET SISTER,
YOU ARE AWESOME!

HAPPY
BIRTHDAY